A Kintsugi Life

Finding Strength and Hope in the Face of Loss

By Kelly Holden

PathBinder
Publishing LLC
COLUMBUS, INDIANA

Published by PathBinder Publishing
P.O. Box 2611
Columbus, IN 47202
www.PathBinderPublishing.com

Edited by Lori Haggard
Covers designed by Kassondra Hattabaugh
Images by iStock, Pixabay, and submitted

First published in 2023
Manufactured in the United States

ISBN: 978-1-955088-70-1
Library of Congress Control Number: 2023917291

Introduction

Kintsugi is a centuries-old Japanese art of repairing broken pottery and transforming it into a network of art with gold. *"Kin"* means "gold," and *"tsugi"* means "joinery." *Kintsugi* pertains to the Zen ideal of *wabi sabi*, the concept of embracing imperfection. It also relates to finding value and beauty in imperfections and blemishes. My life, like many others, resembles broken pottery. I think the key to being happy is finding beauty in these imperfections.

This is my story of loving two people immensely and understanding that finding love again does not mean you stop loving the first person in any way. It is a story of grief, healing, and hope.

When I met my first husband, Nick, I heard "you are so lucky" many times. I *was* lucky. He was such an amazing person that I cannot adequately express it, but those who knew him know it is true. However, he tragically died at age 46 from cancer, and this completely shattered my world. I was not sure I would recover, but I eventually did with a lot of work, prayer, love, and help. I met my second husband, Keith, on this journey and learned so much about grief, hope, and love. I want to share my journey in hopes that I can help someone else. Life and love are hard, but they can also be beautiful.

I recently heard movie producer Judd Apatow state in an interview with best-selling author Brené Brown that the greatest gift you can give others is your story. So here is mine.

Table of Contents

The Beginning

I met Nick at Franklin College in 1986. I was a freshman, and he was a junior. He played basketball and baseball and was an art major. It is an odd combination to be an athlete and artistic, but this applied to so many in his family who were talented in many ways. He was also intimidating to me. I was a quiet person who'd moved to this small college and knew no one. During my freshman year of college, I rarely said a word to him. At the end of the year, I attended a dance with someone else, but Nick asked me to dance. I was so nervous; I hardly said a word. Then we left campus for the summer, and I went home to Cincinnati.

The following fall, Nick and I had a biology class together. One day after class, he asked me out. Not surprisingly, he had flowers delivered to my room before our date and then brought me more the day of our date. The first ones had not even died!

We went on our first date, and Nick did most of the talking. I just kept wondering why in the world he would ask me out. I honestly thought we did not have much in common, but the more I got to know him, the more I realized we did have a lot in common, and our differences were a good complement to each other.

We had no money, but we were both willing to work hard and invest in our future. At one point, Nick told me he wanted six children, and I told him that I would compromise at three. However, we were both excited to start a family.

Those first few years were a lot of fun. We spent a lot of time with family and friends. I decided to attend law school but needed to do it at night while working full time during the day to pay the tuition. Nick was a champion and took care of everything at home while I worked and went to school. He also played in a lot of sports leagues and worked as a graphic artist, both of which he loved.

Nick was larger than life— six foot seven inches tall, handsome, and always smiling. I thought he was gorgeous. For sure, these are great characteristics, but not why I married him. I married him because he was truly one of the nicest people I have ever met. He loved me and loved his family. He always did what was right and was such a unique person. He made me feel like I was the most important person in the world. He was incredible. His life was far too short, and he suffered more than anyone should.

September 1996

Nick had a history of Crohn's Disease for almost nine years, and over the preceding five months, he had lost 30 pounds and barely had energy to work his normal eight-hour shift as a graphic artist. He had quit playing all the sports he loved—basketball, softball, and even golf—due to a lack of energy. He had seen numerous physicians, and they ran him through a battery of tests to no avail.

By September, Nick was anemic and had been receiving shots to boost his red blood cells, but they were not working. His doctors did a colonoscopy, drew blood work, and ran other tests, but were stumped. He went from being this very handsome, outgoing, and energetic person to being almost bedridden and depressed. In hindsight, it was fairly obvious what the problem was, but we did not find out until almost too late.

September 29, 1996, was a beautiful fall day. It was warm and sunny. My father had tickets to the Bengals football game and invited me to go with him as he occasionally did. I always loved the games and spending time with him, but I had to say no. Then my mother called and asked me to go shopping with her, but again I said no. Nick had been feeling ill for several months now, and I was afraid to leave him alone at that point.

Later that day on September 29, he yelled for me and was writhing in extreme pain, unable to breathe. I was terrified and called 911. He was in so much pain he could not even walk. I had no idea what was going on at the time, but I was afraid that he was dying and felt terrible for his intense pain. When we arrived at the hospital, the ER was packed, and the staff was clearly overwhelmed. The doctor was rushed and told me that Nick had "free air" in his diaphragm. I had no idea what that meant at the time. He then explained that Nick's bowel had perforated, and he needed emergency surgery. It was now Sunday evening.

A Kintsugi Life

Nick's condition was so serious that he was transferred to another hospital with a surgical team waiting. It was a surreal moment—standing in the ER with him vomiting and a young ER doctor asking me if I had a surgeon for him. I was 28, and Nick was 30. So, no, we did not have a surgeon on call. The surgeon at the next hospital briefed me that his condition was serious, and he was going to do the best he could to save his life. I asked him not to do a colostomy bag because Nick was an athlete and played a lot of sports. Kindly, he looked at me and said, "I need you to consent to whatever I need to do in order to save his life." I knew, then, that I was not fully grasping the issues at hand, and I began sobbing. This was completely unreal, and I was alone in a hospital with my husband now in emergency surgery. I was terrified.

Nick's mother was an ER nurse and working a shift in Indianapolis two hours away. I was able to reach her on the hospital payphone and kept her briefed through a long night of surgery. This was before cell phones, so I had to call her hospital's main number and ask for her to be paged. I eventually reached my family, too, and they came to sit with me. This would be one of many times they sat in a hospital with me while we waited.

Hours later when he came out of surgery, I was told that he had two perforations and his bowel wall had blown apart. Further, his lymph nodes were the size of potatoes. These were all terms and body parts I was not entirely familiar with, so I had to learn fast. Nick had a colostomy bag because they could not re-connect the bowels. I was told it would be temporary, but for now he needed to heal, and it would be a long road. His infection was so bad they could not sew him closed, so he had something called "second-intention healing," healing without surgical intervention. When I told his mother all of this, her exasperation and comments that this was "not good" added to the weight I was feeling.

I went to my mom's house, as I didn't want to be alone at my house, to get some sleep and returned to the hospital early the next day. I had predictably failed at getting sleep, but knew I needed to try to rest as much as I could. Nick did not wake up for several days, so we just sat and watched him while being briefed by all the doctors.

Nick's mother came to town, and her first comment was that Nick's condition was the worst she had seen. She was an experienced ER nurse who dealt with gun and knife wounds regularly, so again—not welcome comments. However, she was always honest and never said much, but when she did, she meant it. The situation was grave.

After a while, I started to deal with the circumstances and became focused on him recovering—Nick getting his colostomy reversed, and us getting on with life. For the prior four years, I had worked full-time and attended law school at night. Work and school had been my life. I had graduated from law school three months prior to September 29, and had taken two bar exams two months earlier, so I was ready to have fun and see my husband again. But that summer had been spent trying to figure out what was wrong with Nick, not celebrating my graduation. And then this happened. I needed to get over this hurdle and move forward.

The News Gets Worse

On October 1, the surgeon came into the room on his normal 6:30 a.m. rounds and sat down, saying he was glad that Nick's mom and I were there. A sinking feeling hit me. You can always tell when someone has bad news, and I felt like I might vomit. To this day I can remember the clothes I was wearing because the memory is so vivid. The doctor went on to say that the pathology showed that Nick had Hodgkin's Disease, and it had spread to his bowel wall. Nick's mom just shook her head and whispered, "Oh, Nick." Just two words, but they carried so much meaning. The surgeon then explained that Nick had stage three cancer, and it was bad. I can recall it like it happened yesterday. I felt like a train hit me. I was screaming in my head, *it has to be wrong!* Nick played two sports in college, did not drink alcohol, and never smoked or did drugs. He was active. He was not the person who was supposed to get cancer at age 30. And how had it progressed to stage three when he'd seen a slew of physicians all summer and had so many tests? Nick was awake enough to hear the news but still in a lot of pain.

The events the rest of that day were a flurry. The oncologist came in and spent a very long time with us. I learned that it is never good if a doctor sits down in your hospital room. It means your condition is serious enough to warrant a longer visit. The oncologist commented that he had never seen Hodgkin's Disease in the bowel, but he could handle it. He also said that, if you had to get cancer, this was the one to get, and it was curable. I remember my aunt showing up for a visit, having no idea that she would be there right after we received this news. She just held me for a while, but I was being strong. I had to be for him.

Then we had to call my mom and deliver the news. She loved Nick like a son, and it killed her to see us all in pain. The oncologist gave us hope and set forth a plan, but first Nick had to recover from surgery, and that road, itself, was a bit long.

When I reflect on those days, it is odd what I remember. For instance, his surgeon was initially very professional but always hurried. After he told Nick that he had cancer and that it looked bad, he never seemed as hurried. In fact, one day he sat on a desk in the room and asked if he could have some of the candy that had been sent to Nick's room. He proceeded to eat candy and just talk. He started to chit chat with us, and this made him seem more human. He became a kind of friend, and Nick grew to really like him. I wish every physician would realize that, if you just spend a few minutes chatting with a patient about non-healthcare related things, it makes a world of difference to the patient and the family.

Nick was released from the hospital a week post-op. During the next week he was home, I was taught by a home health nurse to do "wet to dry dressings" for his incision. I had to sterilize gauze with a solution to clean his incision and then, using gloves and not touching the dry dressing, put that over his incision. I was very nervous doing these and really had no idea what I was doing. I was also taught how to clean his stoma and empty his colostomy bag. I had never heard of a stoma, which was essentially his bowel sewn to the outside of his stomach. It was not a pretty sight, and all of the sudden I was learning how to care for him.

I had just graduated from law school, was trying to start my career as a lawyer, and suddenly in way over my head doing medical caretaking of a cancer patient. I kept asking for a home health nurse to do all of this, but insurance was not having it, so I did the best I could. I also had to give him injections for his low blood counts, something I was not trained to do. I cannot say that I always did them correctly. I spent many nights crying myself to sleep and being scared out of my mind. I was completely overwhelmed.

Nick became very sick again the following week and lost 30 more pounds, putting his weight at 155 pounds. He was now dangerously thin for his height and build. His healthy weight was 230 pounds, and that was still thin for him. I kept calling the physicians but did not get much response. Nick's mother predicted that he had abscesses, which were pockets of infection from the bowel perforation. Finally, our family doctor had Nick readmitted to the hospital. They drained liters of fluid from his abdomen due to abscesses. He underwent a procedure in radiology to have tubes inserted to drain his abscesses. This was one of many instances where doctors were baffled and did not listen. I learned to be insistent with help from my mother-in-law and other medical family members.

Nick spent another week in the hospital due to the abscesses. The surgeon tried to send him home with drains coming out of his abdomen, but I drew the line there. It was already scary enough. No way was I going to handle that! Nick agreed and felt safer in the hospital. Thankfully, they kept him until the drains were removed.

The Chemo Road

After several weeks, we had a long visit with his oncologist who did an extensive history and a bone marrow biopsy, one of many Nick would have in his life. I had to step out of the room for the procedure. I'm pretty sure if I'd watched it, I would have passed out. I was strong to a point, but knew my limits. His mom stayed in the room and held his hand. The biopsy showed that the cancer was not in his bones, just his bowel and blood. Finally, some good news! A plan was set forth to start chemotherapy. He was given a strong combination of chemo drugs, but we were told it would cure him. Due to his weakened condition from a surgery that had cut him from sternum to groin and a massive infection, he had to wait to start chemo until he regained some physical strength.

While this was sinking in for the next several days, I asked a doctor on call about having children. We had been trying for several months before he got sick. The doctor merely shook his head and said that would not happen. The chemo would make him sterile. He also warned us that the Hodgkin's could kill him. There was no guarantee that Nick would live, particularly since he was already at stage three. After this very unhappy news, the physician walked out of the room. We not-so-lovingly referred to him as "Dr. Death" for the next 16 years.

Then we cried all over again. Brutal honesty from physicians with no glimmer of hope is hard to hear. It was one more blow and another reason to grieve. People often think of grief in terms of death, but you can grieve over many things, such as losing the ability to have children. Years later, I still grieve about this and always will.

A few days later as I was helping Nick walk around the hospital hallways, he told me that I should leave him and move on with life. Nick was always thinking of others before himself, and this comment was not surprising. I asked him, if I was the one with cancer, would he leave me?

Of course not, he said. When I married him, I was in for the long haul. There was no way would I leave the person I loved most in this world at the time he needed me most. I admit, Nick being near death with cancer at 30 was not what I imagined when I promised "in sickness and in health," but that was where we were.

Nick needed so much care: constant shots to improve his anemia and white blood cell count, dressing changes, and numerous doctor's appointments. For about a month, Nick's mom stayed at our house during the week and went home to work her weekend shifts. This allowed me to go to work when I could, knowing that my income would be the only one some weeks, and we had bills to pay that would now include massive medical bills. Our insurance at the time was not good, and the bills amounted to thousands of dollars. It killed me to leave him and go into the office, but there was little choice. I knew he was in good hands with his mom, though it pained her to watch her son go through all he went through.

Nick was a person you did not forget if you met him. His nickname was "the gentle giant." He was so kind and genuine and filled with integrity. Without a doubt, he changed my life and me for the better. To watch everything he was going through was difficult and unfair. I was so angry and cried a lot of tears, but never in front of Nick. He was my best friend and the person I shared everything with. Suddenly, at the worst moment of my life, I could not share my fear and concerns with him. I was trying to be positive around him, but it felt like I was lying to him every moment. The range of emotions I was experiencing was chaotic and exhausting.

Six months of chemotherapy ensued, and it coincided with long, dreary winter days. The chemo treatments would completely wipe out his white blood cells, making him highly susceptible to infection and killing any energy he had. This would last from 10 days to two weeks, and he would go days without a shower or leaving our couch. No one could visit during those days, making it seem longer. My father paid for cable television in our house so we'd have more than four channels. We were not able to afford it at the time. We were paying off college loans, starting to pay law school loans, and the medical bills were mounting at an alarming rate. My parents also bought us a bigger television since we were still using one I had from my college days. Nick's mom bought us a home computer to give him something else to do. Those things became

Nick's only entertainment during the days that I worked and no visitors were allowed. *The Rosie O'Donnell Show* was the highlight of his days when he was awake enough to watch it.

Christmas came, but it did not feel joyous. Nick was bald by then but had gained a bit of weight. He was in an upswing of a chemo cycle, so we were able to go to my mom's house on Christmas Day. Unfortunately, his colostomy bag broke, causing a large mess and incredible embarrassment for him. I had to run home for extra clothes while he showered. He was mortified. This was not the first, nor would it be the last time this happened, even after his colostomy was reversed. In those moments, my heart just ached for him.

After the bowel heals from the initial surgery, they reconnect the bowel. They did this in April 1997. Nick still had enough healthy bowel to connect it.

Looking back over our journey, I am still amazed at the generosity of others and how much help we had. The employees at Duro Bag where Nick worked donated $1,400 to us, and I was able to pay some medical bills and buy a few small gifts. Without their gesture of kindness, that would not have been possible. None of the employees made a lot of money, and to think they loved him enough to try to make things better was just amazing. When I think back to everything people did for us, it is overwhelming and hard not to see such greatness in this world.

A Kintsugi Life

More Complications

January arrived, and it was the halfway point of Nick's chemotherapy. A PET scan and CT scan were ordered. PET scans were new then, and he was too tall for the machine. It took them a lot of time to figure out how to scan such a tall person. After the PET scan, we had another big meeting with his oncologist. Nick was wearing baggy sweatpants because his right leg was so swollen that he could not get other pants on. It was also incredibly painful. He pulled up his sweats to show his doctor who remarked that a CT scan of his abdomen had shown he had DVT (deep venous thrombosis or a blood clot) in his leg. This was concerning, but that was happily overshadowed by good test results! The CT also showed that there was no visible evidence of cancerous tumors, and the medicine seemed to be working. We had passed another huge hurdle.

A few weeks later, Nick was in such pain again, we went to the ER. He always managed to have his emergencies on the weekends, which was never good. I learned that hospitals sort of shut down on weekends; the staff is limited, some tests are simply not available, and doctors are scarce. This always concerned me and, to this day, I do not understand it at all. A young ER resident saw him and diagnosed him with a "need to pee" and catheterized him. When the extreme pain did not subside, another physician came in and ordered a CT scan which revealed a bowel obstruction, meaning nothing was passing through his bowels. The young resident came back and put a small nasogastric intubation tube down his nose into his stomach. Nick's surgeon came into the room and said surgery would be necessary. The worse news was that they would have to remove the NG tube because it proved too small to relieve the gas from his stomach. When he was on NG tube, he was not fed any food because his bowel was closed shut. However, your body still produces gases that need to be relieved. So, he needed a larger NG tube. This set Nick off more than the thought of impending surgery. The look on his face told me the procedure was barbaric. It was painful to watch. His mood became immediately dark, and he was furious with the resident who clearly was not ready to see patients, much less a complicated cancer patient.

That week, they put a filter in his vena cava one morning for his blood clots, and he had surgery for his bowel obstruction a few hours later in the afternoon. Despite all of this, his spirits improved as the week went on. He was released with another set of scars, but feeling positive about his recovery. A few days later, I went to Lexington to take my third bar exam. Nothing like a little stress all compounded!

Life Goes On

Our spring went by without any more huge medical issues. Nick moved forward with chemotherapy and just pushed through the down weeks. During this time, my sister got married and Nick's brother got married. I always struggled with the fact that life went on for everyone else, while ours seemed on hold waiting to see if his treatment would be successful and if he would survive. It was hard to go to these celebratory events while I was scared out of my mind. I hope that I faked it all pretty well.

I recall being at a Saint Patrick's Day party with family friends. The house was packed with people having fun, and I felt like I was on an island watching everyone from afar. I could not help thinking, how many other people here are wondering how long their spouse will be alive? I was 28 years old, and most people were far older than me—another unfair irony. While standing there, my friend (who was hosting the party) asked me how we were doing. I smiled and gave the pat answer, "Doing fine." He looked at me for a minute and said, "Really, how are you?" Then, I cried.

I still cry when I think about this. Most people do not have the stomach for the real answer to this question, but his wife had been through breast cancer, so he got it. That was one of the moments that I recall vividly when someone really cared and reached out to me. I always felt bad crying or worrying about myself when Nick was the one physically going through all of the pain and agony. Caregivers go through a lot, but complaining or feeling bad for your own plight seems selfish when someone you love is physically and emotionally suffering so much.

Cancer Support Groups

One of my saving graces during this journey was our cancer support group. My friend and his wife started this at our church, and I so looked forward to the meetings. Family and friends felt bad for us, but only those with cancer or their caregivers really understood the pain. I learned that, for me, finding a group that could help us was vital to getting through these times. That was a lesson I would not forget. I encourage anyone to find a support group or system if you go through something like this.

During one of our group meetings, a resource nurse recommended a book entitled *All Things Work for Good: A Book of Encouragement for People with Cancer, Their Family and Friends* by Gavin Sinclair. I devoured this book and reached out to the author, Gavin. Surprisingly, he and his wife wrote back. Gavin had been diagnosed with cancer at age 24, and their journey felt a lot like ours. I had the opportunity to meet Gavin and his wife, Jennifer, and hear him speak about his journey, which I found very helpful. The fact that they took time to talk with us and answer questions was incredible.

The End of Chemo

Nick had a planned surgery on April 28, one day after our six-year wedding anniversary. I recall him smiling in the hospital bed saying this was the happiest day of his life. He was done with chemotherapy, and his colostomy, which he despised, was being reversed. He was tired of feeling terrible; it had been almost a year since he started feeling very sick.

His surgery was to reverse his colostomy, do a final staging (biopsy) of organs to see if the cancer was gone, and do a splenectomy, which was done then for Hodgkin's patients; it's not done any more. His surgeon warned us that removal of his spleen would affect his immune system, and if he ran a fever in the future to immediately take him to the ER and tell them that he had no spleen (This would happen more than I believed it would). Nick was ecstatic the morning of his surgery to eliminate his colostomy bag. He hated it more than I can describe.

Surgery took almost five hours, and he was returned to his room in extreme pain. All his scar tissue from previous surgeries made it difficult to remove his spleen, and the surgeon informed me that he had to tug and tug to get it out, causing significant swelling and subsequent pain. It was agonizing to watch Nick in so much pain, which was almost unbearable. The pain lasted for several days until medicine finally made the swelling go down.

Recovery

The best news was that his pathology came back clean. He was cancer free and really on the road to recovery. It was a slow process, but he healed with tenacity. When he was physically able, he started lifting weights and working out. He was determined to gain back weight and muscle tone.

Nick had lived his life as an athlete, and laying around for almost a year was not tolerable. Within a few months, he was back to a good weight. Our friends and family were amazed at his transformation. His hair regrew, and he looked back to his old self.

One good side effect of chemo is that his Crohn's Disease also went into remission which allowed him to eat and gain weight for the first time in years. That summer after he healed, we spent tons of time with family and friends. Being able to go out again and not be sheltered in our house was such a huge blessing.

Having a Family

Our focus now was on having a family. We had been trying when Nick was sick, but we knew that his chemotherapy would make this difficult, if not impossible—something else that cancer took from us. We started looking at adoption. We debated whether we should wait to adopt to be sure he was cancer free for a period of time.

His physician warned us to wait because Hodgkin's has a high recurrence rate. But we decided that we had waited long enough for life to begin, that no one knows when the end will come, and living in such fear was not an option. So, we moved forward with the good side of life.

Unexpectedly, we had an opportunity to adopt a baby girl through a family friend. It was fast and sudden and clearly a gift from God. Six months after Nick's last surgery, we watched our daughter, Meghan, be born. She was born on October 31 and was beautiful. Suddenly, we were a family. We had gone from such a low point to a high point so quickly, it made our heads spin.

Our lives went from being dark and scary to being wonderful!

Meghan was a great baby who was always happy. It was hard to believe our good fortune. When Meghan was two, she was diagnosed with hemiplegic cerebral palsy. Initially it was a blow to us, and I mourned for all the things she could not physically do. However, she was a brilliant child who was verbal and hilarious from an early age. Her CP required a lot of testing and therapy, but in some ways, it seemed minor compared to what Nick had been through.

Then we talked about having another child. A little over three years later, our son, Brendan, was born. My wish to be pregnant and have a baby was fulfilled. Brendan was a sweet baby and toddler, always hugging and loving on us. Our life had done a total 180, and it was hard to believe that, after being in such a dark and scary place for over a year, we were finally living the life we had dreamed about.

Career Change

Life moved on, and eventually, Nick fulfilled his lifelong dream of being a teacher. He went back to school at the University of Cincinnati to obtain his Master of Art Education.

He had been hesitant to do this for years, but my career as a lawyer was going well, so I told him to pursue his dream. It was a bit scary for him to quit his job as a graphic artist so that he could student teach (for no money), but it was what had to be done.

He finished his student teaching, and within two months, he had a job at a school five minutes from our house. It was perfect for him, and he loved the job. The students loved him. He brought 13 years of real-world experience working as an artist with him to the job and had amazing lesson plans. We could not go anywhere in public without seeing his students who just adored him.

Nick's teaching position allowed him a lot of time off to rest when needed and to take care of the kids. He was with them on all breaks, snow days, all summer, etc. They were blessed to have quality time with their dad that many kids do not experience.

I worked a lot trying to build a law practice, and his schedule allowed me to do so and be the primary breadwinner. I envied his time with the kids, but our roles were defined, and I knew he needed a job with time off for his health.

Crohn's Disease Returns

As time progressed, Nick's health began to deteriorate, and we had several scares. He went often for routine testing, and numerous PET scans showed inflammation and potential cancer. However, none of those panned out after further testing. I learned to dread the routine PET or CT scans.

When Nick turned 39, his Crohn's Disease came back, and it did so with a vengeance. His gastroenterologist in Cincinnati was very concerned about how to treat it because many of the medications can potentially cause lymphoma, which he'd already had. We were sent to the University of Chicago to see a specialist who told us we had to medicate it and take the risk of lymphoma because living with untreated Crohn's was not an option. Nick tried infusions of a drug called Remicade. The infusions were every two weeks and could be no later than 2 p.m., requiring him to take leave from work and causing scheduling problems. After 18 months, the Remicade was not working and was discontinued, and he was placed on a new drug, Humira. It helped with symptoms but was not perfect.

Nick's Crohn's Disease would get so out of control that his bowel would swell shut and cause obstructions. He had three obstructions in four years which were incredibly painful and required him to be hospitalized for multiple days. These were exceedingly stressful days when I was juggling my work, the kids with school and activities, and being at the hospital to help him. None of the obstructions required surgery, thankfully, but he needed large doses of steroids to stop the swelling.

More Health Complications

In 2008, during one of Nick's hospital stays, he'd contracted C. difficile (commonly known as C. diff.), a nasty infection that is common in older people in nursing homes. It is highly contagious and dangerous. This made him very sick and required another hospital stay. From that day forward, his hospital charts always had a big "C. diff" notation on the front, like the scarlet letter.

He also had ongoing battles with blood clots. His hematologist said his blood was like jelly, it was so thick. He was placed on high doses of a blood thinner, Coumadin, which required bi-weekly blood draws at the hematologist's office, which was a good 20-25-minute drive from our house. Our children were frequently with him for these and became friends with all the nurses. At times, Nick was too busy to have this done and would go for weeks without having his blood checked or Coumadin readjusted but would never tell me. This resulted in his blood either being too thick or too thin, both of which are bad. We ended up in the ER several times when he could not breathe due to tiny clots that had formed in his lungs. It was a roller coaster of healthcare.

Nick also had vascular problems that required two surgeries, one on each leg. Working with surgeons who will not listen is always fun and, after one surgery, he clotted from his knee to ankle and was in extreme pain as a result. I learned that minor procedures were never minor for him. I also learned that, when the physicians would not listen or take time to understand his complicated history, disaster could ensue.

He had deep vein thrombosis in his right leg from his initial cancer, and that caused his leg to swell every day. In the last seven or eight years of his life, Nick wore compression hose to keep the swelling down. The hose were hot and uncomfortable and did not entirely work. He also developed venous stasis ulcers on his ankles like a diabetic, and those frequently became infected. These ulcers looked like massive bruises and affected the integrity of his skin. People often asked him how he bruised himself because they looked so bad and painful. Our list of specialty doctors grew, and Nick and I both learned a lot about healthcare, including the good, the bad, and (at times) the very ugly.

Additionally, Nick suffered from significant nerve damage (neuropathy) in his feet; on some days, the pain was unbearable. This was another side effect of chemo. He said he never was pain free any day without taking Vicodin, which was a strong painkiller. But he knew that Vicodin was addictive so only took it when absolutely necessary. Doctors tried numerous medications and testing, but the result was that he had permanent nerve damage. It could not be repaired. He just had to live with it and deal with the pain.

Nick was an athlete and a happy guy who could now hardly get off the couch some days, or might be stuck in the hospital. At times, when the multitude of problems was overwhelming, Nick would sink into a depression. To the outside world, he was awesome. He did not show this side to anyone but me. I was saddled with all other responsibilities of our life and tried to keep him on track mentally. It was my burden to carry, and it was a lot most days. Nick had changed so much from all these health problems, and I could not blame him one bit. I was angry for him that this had happened and just tried to love and support him any way I knew how.

2013-The Worst Year

In 2013, our kids were in fifth grade and ninth grade, smack in the middle of busy years with sports, activities, and school. Nick had a newer job that he loved teaching high school art. My career was very busy. Nick's near-constant health issues aggravated him to no end and were a great source of stress for us both.

Nick spent a lot of time with our kids. Meghan was the artsy kid, so he helped with school plays and got her to all her vocal ensemble practices. Brendan was the sporty kid, so Nick coached him in football and basketball. Truly, Nick was one of the best coaches I have ever seen for kids. He spent endless hours planning plays and figuring out how to help the kids improve. He also wanted it to be fun, so he made up nicknames for the kids and designed t-shirts that he gave to them. He wanted every kid to feel special and part of the team. His patience was unmatched. Although he couldn't play any longer, he channeled his love for sports into coaching, and it showed.

In February of 2013, Brendan's fifth-grade basketball team made it into the final four for the Catholic Youth Organization tournament. This was further than the team had ever gone. Nick was ecstatic. During the tournament, he had excruciating pain in his leg where his ulcer was. This was not too concerning as it often got infected, and antibiotics and pain meds usually got him through. Several years earlier, he'd needed IV antibiotics for almost two weeks, and I'd had to get him back and forth to his hematologist for those treatments.

This time, the pain was more intense than in the past.

Nick had multiple visits to the doctor and was using pain meds to get through his days of work and coaching. Brendan's team eventually lost that final four game, but it had been a great season for us. Nick was so proud of those boys and that team.

Then Nick took a turn for the worse and started running a fever. Despite this, he went to school to teach because he hated missing work, but the school nurse made him go home due to his fever. I was scheduled to go out of town with friends, and Nick was scheduled to take Brendan to the Pacers game in Indianapolis. Nick convinced me that he was fine, and we should both continue with our plans. I was very hesitant because he was spiraling downhill. But Nick was adamant, so I went two hours away for a weekend with a group of friends. The doctors were scheduling several tests for the following week, so nothing much was going to happen that weekend, anyway.

Nick left a couple hours after I did to drive Brendan to the Pacers game with his AAU basketball program. When he arrived in Indianapolis, his hematologist called him and told him on the phone that there were "blasts" in his blood. She said this could be a sign of leukemia and wanted him to come in Monday morning for a bone marrow biopsy. Nick called me and told me that his doctor wanted a bone marrow biopsy, but did not tell me about the blasts or possible leukemia. I was immediately alarmed. The last time he had a bone marrow biopsy was when he had Hodgkin's Disease. This seemed like an extreme test for a leg infection. The more I questioned Nick about it, the more irritated he became. He assured me that it was no big deal and would be fine.

I recall sitting and staring into space after the call and someone asking me if I was worried. I had this sense that this was the calm before the storm and things were about to change—and not for the better. I stayed for the weekend primarily because I had driven and would leave people stranded if I left. That was a decision that I would regret for the rest of my life, and I will never overcome the guilt.

I could not wait to get home on Sunday. When I did, Nick told me the truth, and I panicked. Nick and, in typical Nick fashion, went to into work to ensure that his lesson plans were in order for the substitute teacher Monday. Nick was never one to share his issues with anyone, and I knew he would never call his family, so I called his sister, Julie, and talked to her and her husband. They were on a date but were both concerned when I told them the news. I had to tell *someone* and knew they would want to know so they could start praying.

As hard as I try, I cannot recall what happened that evening after he got back from work. It was Nick's last real night at home, and I have no idea what we did, what we talked about, or what the kids were doing. There is nothing in my memory about it. It still makes me sad.

Testing Reveals Leukemia

The next morning, we took the kids to school and showed up at the hospital for his biopsy. I recall that he had a cardiologist appointment later that day and a CAT scan scheduled in afternoon. I remember sitting in the waiting area—Nick was wearing a red pullover with a golf logo, and he looked relaxed and handsome as usual. His hematologist came out, and they took him back for his biopsy. I sat outside and waited until it was over. I never could stomach any of those biopsies; they seemed barbaric, and I am still amazed that there is not an easier way to do those tests.

When I came into the room, his hematologist explained that there were "blasts" in his blood, and she suspected leukemia, but it could be other things as well and not to worry. I had no idea what blasts were, but from how she said it, I knew it was not good or normal. Her comment, not to worry, was not truthful because this was very concerning, as I later found out. Because Nick was struggling to breathe a bit and he had so many tests scheduled for the afternoon, she decided on the spot to admit him. Although this was a good idea, we were blindsided by this and not prepared. He had no extra clothes, and it completely changed the day. I had to get the kids after school and had no plan in place for that.

Nick was admitted on March 18, and all the testing began. In some ways, I think Nick was relieved to get some medical attention as he had been struggling more than he'd let on. I had to go home and tell the kids that he was in the hospital again. I had convinced myself that his blood work results were due to another infection in his legs. I stopped in at my work to pick up some files and told them I would be back once we figured this out.

The next day I went back to the hospital, and my brother-in-law, Micah, showed up. We were sitting on the couch chatting with Nick who still felt and looked decent. Then his hematologist came into the room along with some nurses. She informed us that the biopsy showed *acute myelogenous leukemia* or "AML." She explained the process for chemotherapy and a stem cell transplant and ordered what seemed like reams of tests. She told us he would need to be in the hospital for at least 30 days.

For the second time in my life, I felt like a train hit me. This was unbelievable. He had already been through so much, and this was unfair beyond belief. I recall looking at my brother-in-law, and tears were streaming down his face. Seeing him cry broke my heart more than anything. It was bad, but we had no idea how much worse it would get.

From there things moved quickly. Chemo started and Nick began getting massive blood clots all over his body. Within days he had his first of many surgeries, called thrombectomies, to break up the clots. My cousin worked in interventional radiology where they did these surgeries and was a godsend during these procedures. Just having someone to sit with me and keep me calm was much needed.

Nick's family came in from Indianapolis, and he assured everyone he would be fine. He had five siblings, surely one of them would be his match. The thought was that he needed 30 days of chemo, some recovery time, and then he would have the transplant. It seemed so easy. People recovered from leukemia all the time, so I thought.

They took blood from him to do a cytogenetics test which would provide more information about his leukemia and, from what I understood, his chance of surviving this. I asked every day when that test would be back. Finally, after two weeks, it was back.

I asked his doctor about it as she was in a rush to leave the room that morning, and she said it was back and not good, but we would discuss it the next day. I told her that tomorrow was Good Friday, our kids were off school, and I could not be there at 7 a.m. for rounds. Therefore, I needed her to share it now so I was with Nick when she explained it. She then quickly told us his leukemia was treatment-induced.

His first chemotherapy for Hodgkin's Disease had caused the leukemia, and he was in the lowest 20 percentile for his cytogenetics test. Essentially, his chance of survival was less than 20 percent. It was devastating. His DNA had been damaged by the chemotherapy 16 years earlier. She later remarked that they now know not to give the chemo he'd received in 1996 because it can cause leukemia. In retrospect, they should never have given it, but it was too late now. The damage was done.

Easter

For Easter weekend, my family and friends took the kids to Lake Cumberland to allow them to have a mini-vacation and to alleviate pressure from me so I could focus on Nick. I spent the entire Easter weekend with him, even sleeping in the hospital. I only went home to shower and get him clothes. He hated it when I left and begged me to come back as soon as I could.

I was constantly torn between caring for our kids and being there for Nick. The kids visited, but it was scary for them to see their dad getting sicker, and it was boring in the hospital. In hindsight, I wish I would have had them come more often and just hang out with him, but we make the best choices we can with the information we know at the time.

One Night Home

We were heavy into the AAU season, and each weekend I would juggle getting our son, Brendan, to games and being at the hospital. I called in favors from friends and family to help Nick pass the time while I went to the games I could. I had been filming all the games to show Nick afterwards. He would then talk with Brendan about what he saw. I recall one time Brendan saying, "I wish dad was there to help me during the games instead of just telling me after."

At one point, Nick came home for one night. Nick's sisters were in town and helped me pack up his room and get him home. Brendan had a basketball game, and we all went. Nick had to wear a mask but sat and yelled at the refs as usual. One ref was so fed up with him, he almost kicked him out. The game Nick saw that night would be the last one he would see in person. Brendan played his heart out and had a great game.

Nick's one night home, which happened to be our 22nd wedding anniversary, was a disaster. They sent a home health nurse to show me how to clean his central line and inject all his medications. She commented that he was on a lot of anticoagulants. The next morning, Nick woke up with a terrible headache. I had to rush him back to the ER. He had a brain bleed. This was his second bleed episode, and they were terrifying.

Nick had dealt with coagulation issues since 1996, and managing them was difficult. His first bleed episode was during the two and a half months in that first hospital. He'd had three brain bleeds and five thrombectomies, meaning his blood was either too thick or too thin. At one point, his physician had asked us what we wanted to do about his coagulation medication, as if *we* had any idea! We were at her mercy, and that was increasingly alarming to both of us.

This time the pain was so severe that he had to be in a dark, quiet room, and he was so medicated that it slowed his breathing. His sisters

A Kintsugi Life

were home with the kids. They cleaned the house then left when my mom showed up to take over kid duties. I spent the night with Nick in the hospital waiting for him to recover from the bleed.

Second Round of Chemo

The initial plan had been for Nick to spend 30 days in the hospital (which seemed like an eternity), and then he'd go home to recover before his bone marrow transplant. No one warned us that the chemo may not work, and more chemo could be in store. After 30 days, they did another biopsy, and the results were the same: blasts in his blood. The chemo was not working, and the leukemia was not in remission. So they shifted gears and gave him another heavy dose of chemo and another 30 days in the hospital.

Although this was a huge setback, Nick handled it with grace and was pretty upbeat. He loved his nurses. He walked several times a day to stay as active as he could in a hospital. They let us leave the floor occasionally and go into the courtyard. The weather was warming up, so I took him outside whenever I could.

He had to wear a mask and, due to his clots, was wrapped up like a mummy at times to suppress the swelling from the clots. At least being outside seemed somewhat normal. He enjoyed those moments, and I used to pretend that things were normal, and we were just sitting outside enjoying the fresh air.

After the second round of chemo, we had to wait a couple of weeks for Nick's blood cells to start producing again to see whether or not the leukemia was in remission. The days until the next bone marrow biopsy were agonizing. That morning I went to Mass, and so did some friends and family. Then I sat in the waiting room praying the rosary while they did the bone marrow biopsy. I still could not stomach being in the room while they did it. As usual, he did not complain and was upbeat.

The results came back on the Friday of Memorial Day weekend. His physician came in and told us that the leukemia remained, and there was nothing else she could do. She planned to release him after the weekend to essentially go home to die. I recall at some point asking about clinical trials because he was not ready to give up. The response from his physician was to ask me whether I was willing to lose our house and everything to pay for a clinical trial. This was shockingly asked in front of Nick, as if I would choose the house over my husband's life. I knew then that it was time for a new physician. We were desperate.

Nick's cousin showed up at the hospital only to find us both crying. I felt terrible for her, and she felt she should leave. I told her that I needed her there to keep him company. So she stayed and spent the afternoon with us, and her presence was a blessing. Nick's sister, Julie, also came in that weekend and spent the night with us at the hospital. I can hardly remember those days, they were so painful, but I recall being grateful that his family was there to share this awful burden and be with him.

Another Care Plan

I was on the phone and sending emails, contacting doctors all over the country to consult and take over his care. I was amazed at how many responded to me and even called me. Several offered to see him and consult on his care. Eventually, I contacted a transplant doctor in Cincinnati who came to see Nick in person and offered to take over his care. He told Nick he would do a transplant even if the leukemia was not in remission. His chances were still about 20 percent, but that beat zero, so we jumped at it. The moment we met this doctor, we were at ease and knew we were in good hands.

Nick was released on a Friday to go home. The plan was to admit Nick to the new hospital the following Monday. I warned the new physician that he would never make it through the weekend at home. He needed platelets and blood every day. Although he was released home, we had to go back to the prior hospital on Saturday for blood work and platelets. We spent eight hours sitting in a room waiting for his platelets to come from the blood bank. It was his last weekend home, and we spent it back in the hospital due to inefficiencies.

That Sunday morning, Nick could not get out of bed. He'd tried and had fallen against the wall. I had to call my neighbor to come help him down the steps. I recall thinking, as we put him into the car to go the emergency room, that this may be the last time he was ever home or slept in his bed. We lived in a two-story house. That night before, I'd tried to get him to sleep on the couch as climbing steps was a challenge, but he'd insisted on sleeping in his own bed. Who could blame him?

I drove Nick to the ER at the new hospital and had a nurse get a wheelchair to get him into the building. He had to wear a mask due to his susceptibility for infection. Once we told them he had leukemia and was supposed to be admitted Monday, things moved along quickly. They got him into a room on the transplant floor, and I was told to move the car. I walked back into the hospital and had no idea how to find his room again. I had spent two and a half months in another hospital and knew every nook and cranny of it, and now we were starting over again. I was trying not to cry with frustration as I was now lost and could not find him.

Immediately, things were very different at Jewish Hospital. The transplant wing was separated by doors from the rest of the hospital. Upon entering, you were required to wash your hands at a huge sink and check in. Jewish Hospital was very protective of its transplant patients and took careful steps to guard against infection. The change was welcome, and I immediately felt better.

On Monday morning, an entire crew of healthcare professionals came into the room, and I learned that they did this every single morning. Their team included the physicians, nurse practitioners, a dietiian, a social worker, and anyone else who needed to be involved. The care was comprehensive and intense.

Each morning we knew the plan and his blood work results. They were all written on a whiteboard as well. Nick immediately started on a massive chemo dose. This caused him to be bedridden and unable to speak as the chemo had made him so weak. They were trying to kill his leukemia, but the process made him very sick as a result. He was initially okay with that, knowing it was his only chance.

We Have a Match!

We had waited for months to find out if he had a sibling who was a match. Finally, they told us that his sister was a 10/10 match, and one of his brothers was a 7/10 match. It was the best news we had heard since his diagnosis. His sister agreed to donate stem cells, and she started her testing for the donation. Nick was convinced that his sister's strong immune system would cure him and asked almost every day, "When do I get her cells?" All his hopes were hanging on her curing him, and he was more than ready.

More Failed Chemo and Heart Problems

As it had been in the past, this round of chemo failed, and then another one. His condition continued to deteriorate. One Saturday morning, I went to the hospital early for rounds and left mid-morning as my cousin was doing a fundraiser for Nick at her restaurant, so I went home to get the kids. Nick's brother and sister were coming to sit with him. I tried never to leave him alone for long. As I pulled into my driveway, the unit clerk called and told me calmly that I needed to come back immediately. She would not tell me what was wrong, but that I just needed to get there.

I was convinced that he had died during my half-hour drive home. Driving back to the hospital was one of my worst drives ever. I was physically shaking as I pulled into the hospital parking lot and had no idea why the unit clerk would not tell me what was wrong. I got there to find his family in a waiting room, and they said no one would tell them anything. I walked into his room to find a lot of staff.

Apparently, his heart rate had gone up to 210, which was bad. I learned that this was not an unusual side effect of chemo, but quite a scary one. Nick had been watching the Master's golf tournament and had no idea that this was going on until they came rushing in with a crash cart. The unit clerk had seen his heart rate on a monitor and called a code. His heart ejection fraction was down to 17 percent, which was also very bad. This prompted a new round of medications, and we added yet another doctor, a cardiologist.

I ended up staying at the hospital for the next 48 hours as I was afraid to leave at that point. On Sunday morning, a cardiologist came in and sat with us for over an hour. He told us that he'd called every couple of hours to check on Nick. He also told us that Nick's case hit very close to home. His wife had Hodgkin's Disease about 19 years prior, and she'd had the same chemo that Nick had, so he had been following Nick's case closely.

At times during our journey, some of the healthcare providers became real people, and I could tell that watching this young and once-vibrant person deteriorate was killing them like it was me. I will never forget that doctor's face and his kindness that morning. He was basically telling us that this sucked, and he felt the pain, too.

Although Nick was physically declining, occasionally I was still seeing glimpses of who he used to be. On Monday, another cardiologist came in to check on his status, another nice guy who was about 80 pounds overweight. After he left the room, Nick looked at me and said, "Really? Did you see how big he is and I'm the one with heart problems?" He just shook his head. I laughed, something I had not done much of lately.

As they continued different chemo treatments, Nick was physically deteriorating, and his waking hours became fewer. His ability to communicate was quickly decreasing. At the end of June, I left the hospital late on a Saturday night and felt terrible. Everything hurt, and I realized I had a fever when I got home. I had a neighbor and some of the family go to the hospital on Sunday, and I went to a doctor on Monday. I had developed a horrible cough and bronchitis.

Due to my fever, I was not able to go to the hospital. I tried to explain to my physician that I needed to get over this as soon as possible because I was the main caregiver for him. I recall her being very unconcerned and in a hurry to get out of the exam room to get to other patients. I had just told her that my husband had leukemia and was on month four in a hospital, and she hardly even expressed any sympathy. I fired her after that visit. I was so angry.

Nick's brother was able to come to town and sit with him until my fever finally broke, but it took four days. It was killing me to be at home and not be with him. He was not in a good place when I could not be there. I used those few days to spend time with the kids. I was able to help Meghan get her temporary driving permit as we were three months behind. I also finally got my hair cut, which was long overdue. This forced time away was a needed break for me and good for the kids, but difficult for Nick. I probably went back before I should have, but I wore a mask and kept my distance until I was completely better.

July 4

July 4 was one of our worst days and a turning point. It was the first time that Nick told me he knew he would not make it. It poured down rain the whole day, and Nick was not able to get out of bed or eat. My side of the family, for the past 20-plus years, always goes to my aunt's cottage for a Fourth of July celebration. So I got the kids ready to go with my family, then I headed to the hospital.

Nick had contracted VRE, which is some type of infection, and, as a result, could not leave his room because he could infect other patients. Being confined to his room, he became so depressed from everything. I felt like he was giving up and told him that. I was crying and telling him he was giving up and was going to leave us alone. He was yelling at me that I had no idea how it felt to be confined to a tiny room, to hurt everywhere, and to know that he was going to die.

Then I went and sat in the lobby and cried because I felt terrible for yelling at him and just had no idea what to do. When I went back in the room, he was on his exercise bike trying to exercise. I just apologized and hugged him for a long time. We both broke that day, and I was ashamed of myself for losing it in front of him.

My sister called me in the evening to check on us, but I was not able to speak to her because I could not stop crying. She came up to the hospital with some of my friends and brought me dinner.

For the next eight days, Nick just worsened. He was bedridden, incontinent, and unable to speak most of the time.

July 12

On July 12, I got to the hospital early, and Nick was struggling to breathe. They had done a chest X-ray at 4 a.m., and it was fine, so they were perplexed. The team came out on rounds, and they started scurrying to help him. Another chest X-ray revealed that his lungs were full of fluid. Around 11, they decided he needed to be intubated to help him breathe. Nick's fifth round of chemo had failed, and they mentioned briefly that they'd been thinking about sending him to the Sarah Cannon Cancer Institute in Nashville, Tennessee. But for now, they needed to focus on his immediate problem, so that plan was set aside.

It hit me that, when they intubated him, he would no longer be able to talk. I told him how much I loved him and that he needed to continue fighting. I asked if the kids should come up so he could talk to them, but he shook his head no. He did not want them to see him like this.

He was shaking badly from struggling to breathe. Then they took him away and said they would come get me once they got him settled. They were moving him to the ICU, so I had to move all of his personal effects into the ICU as he was being discharged from his room. I was frantically trying to call my family, but I was getting voicemail all around.

Our son was with friends at a movie, but I needed the kids to be at the hospital. I called Nick's family and told them they may want to come into town. I was not sure what in the world to do. I recall Nick's aunt, Randi, calling me because I had done a quick Facebook post. The next few hours were a blur, but family started rushing in. Soon the waiting room was full. Nick was intubated and unaware of who was around. They had paralyzed him from the neck down so that he would not struggle to breathe over the machines.

Nick seemed to stabilize, but he looked scary hooked up to all the machines. The oncologist came in and told me he was doing better and, in the morning, we would discuss a plan for his next treatment and to transplant his sister's stem cells. It all sounded positive, and then I felt bad having his family drive in two hours for a false alarm. Because the ICU could only have a few people at a time, I went to the waiting room to let his family spend time with him. Then his sister Julie came to get me and said I needed to come to his room right away.

I had the kids brought to hospital right after he was admitted to ICU and they stayed several hours. Once they thought he was stabilized, family took them home.

Codes and Crash Carts

Nick's heart rate was dropping, and the respiratory therapist and nurses were calling for a crash cart. Then they called a code and people came running from everywhere. The ICU had a glass wall and door, so we stood there for two hours while they revived him, only for his heart rate to drop again, and they'd do it all over again. Thankfully, I had sent the kids home when he stabilized, so they did not witness this. A young doctor came to me and told me that I had to tell them when to stop. She explained that he was not breathing, and when his respirations got too low, his heart stopped. I asked her if she could save him, and she shook her head no. Then I was angry. Why was she asking me this question and having me make this decision? I still do not understand it.

Some people describe death as a peaceful journey. I have heard stories about people suddenly waking up and smiling or seeing angels. This is not what I saw. I saw blood and healthcare workers sweating and crying and all of us just sobbing. It was not peaceful. Because Nick's lungs were filling with blood, when they were resuscitating him, blood was squirting out of his respirator and going all over his face and the gowns on the workers. When we stepped into his room, Nick's brother said a prayer. Nick was breathing, but barely. I whispered to him how sorry I was and that I loved him. I also told him it was okay to go as I knew he was in pain, and that we would be fine. I left like I had just lied to him, but I knew he needed to go. I have no idea what possessed me to say this to him, but I felt he needed to hear from me that it was okay to be at peace. Within a minute after I whispered to him, he was gone. They could not save him. Thankfully the kids were not there to see it.

I asked the nurse to clean him up, and we collected all his belongings and left the hospital.

The Aftermath

Now I had the hard job of going home to tell both the kids that their dad had died. I felt physically sick, and I just had no idea how I would ever go on. The life I'd had for 26 years had just ended. Nick was the only person I'd ever loved. He had fought so hard, and he was dead at age 46. I was furious and scared. I called a cousin who owned a funeral home to tell him that I needed his help. I did not know what else to do but make plans.

My mind was going a thousand miles a minute, so I was asking my sister silly questions like, "How long do I keep wearing my wedding ring?" I also remember asking her if I was still married since he had just died. I just cried all the way home. I do not know how she even drove me as she loved him as well.

My sister drove me to my friend's house to pick up Brendan. I had to tell him that his dad did not make it and was at peace. He was 11, and it was the worst moment of his young life and so unfair. Then I had to go to home to tell Meghan. She came out of the house to meet me on the lawn. When I told her, she started screaming at the top of her lungs. My friend two doors down could hear her screaming.

Most of my family and Nick's family were there. We were all crying hard just watching Meghan in so much pain. It was awful. I just held her and told her we would get through it.

My house was full of family, and the moment was just surreal. Looking back years later, that night was a blur. Most of them stayed for the weekend. I tried to sleep and kept waking with nightmares. I was up early and just cried in the shower where no one could hear me. The pain was physical and emotional, and it was unbearable. I had no idea how I was going to raise our kids, work, take care of the house, or do anything.

Then more family and friends started to show up, and food appeared from everywhere. It was summer, so our pool was open, and kids were swimming. It was complete chaos, but it was distracting and good in some ways. I did not want to be alone. They were there to grieve with us and share the pain. I was very thankful for all of them.

Two days before Nick died, Brendan had had surgery to have a screw removed from his elbow that was used to pin his fracture from playing football. He was having an allergic reaction to the bandage, and it was causing hives and itching. With everything going on, he had not been able to tell me. So, on top of having my husband just die, I now had to handle surgical complications with my son. Meghan was supposed to take a test for her driving class that weekend, but she obviously missed that. Life had not gone on that weekend; it had stopped for all of us.

In those last months of Nick's life, friends and family did almost all my grocery shopping, my laundry, the cleaning, and babysitting. I recall a neighbor saying that she kept thinking, as she was folding my under-wear, "We will be very close after this!" I truly could not have gotten through it without these people. They brought food three times a week, gave us endless gift cards, and much more. I sat down multiple times to write thank you notes and did not even know where to start.

Years later there are hundreds of thank you notes that I still owe people. The blessing in all of this was knowing that Nick was so loved that people came from everywhere to help in any way they could. It was truly an amazing outpouring of love and support. Nick was a beloved teacher, and his students' artwork covered his hospital room walls. The school put orange ribbons on the trees outside the school and huge signs. He was even on the news for the support of his students. The broadcast made him and his nurses cry.

The Funeral

The next week was filled with planning a funeral, which was completely surreal. I hardly slept that week. I would wake up in the middle of the night crying and sweating and reliving Nick dying over and over. Then I would panic about how I was going to raise two children alone and what I was going to do alone for the rest of my life. I had a physical pain in my chest that would not go away. I had no idea that grief could be so crushing and physical.

I knew Nick would not want a formal funeral with everyone wearing suits and crying. I asked people to wear orange, which is the color for leukemia, or the shirts that Nick had designed for the kids. I could not handle a visitation and funeral over two days, or being in a funeral home, so I combined them and did a visitation at the church and funeral Mass immediately after. There were probably over 500 people at the funeral. The line was out the church in the parking lot, and people stood in it. We had pictures, artwork, and videos for people to look at while standing in line. To this day, I am not even sure where it all came from, but it just showed up, and I was grateful.

During this time I had this sense that, once the funeral was over, everyone else would go back to their normal lives, but we would not. I knew it in my soul, and it broke my heart for me and my kids. On the Sunday after his funeral, the last of Nick's family left. I closed the door and my daughter said, "Do you think we will ever see them again?" They lived two hours away, and she was afraid, without her dad, they would disappear, too. I assured her that would never happen and, thankfully, they are still very much in our lives.

Summer Break

I took six weeks off work to spend the rest of summer break with my kids. I had not seen them much while Nick was sick, and I knew their grief was immense like mine. I needed to be there all I could. I cried constantly, and it was exhausting.

I also needed to tend to the business side of death. This required making calls almost every day to make all the claims and handle estate-related matters. I did this in the mornings while my kids slept so they did not hear me. I also had to go to the social security office, and to handle the financial side of his dying. Being a lawyer, I was pretty organized, but nothing can prepare you for what is required after your spouse tragically dies.

Two weeks after Nick's death, we took an impromptu trip to the beach. People had been very generous, and every day people dropped off food and our mailbox was filled with cards. Meghan said it was all so nice, but she needed a break. She asked if we could leave Cincinnati for a while because everywhere we turned there was a reminder of her dad. So, we packed three cars full of family and kids and drove to the beach. We were with my sister and her family and my best friend and her family. The week in Hilton Head was exactly what we needed. It was hard suddenly being on a vacation without Nick, but anywhere I went it was hard. We were all grieving, but we were doing it together.

Cincinnati has a phenomenal grief group designed for children called Fernside, so Brendan and I started attending those groups. The drive there the first night was hard. I was sick to my stomach and nervous. However, once we got there, we were put into groups by age. I learned that being with others who have a similar experience is unmatched. It was the saving grace for both of us. My daughter wanted nothing to do with it initially. She was a sophomore in high school and just wanted to go back to school and try to blend in.

A Kintsugi Life

My sister, brother-in-law, and their two kids had moved into my house in June to help care for my kids when they got out of school for the summer, and she offered to stay for a while. I gladly welcomed it as I needed so much help. This was another saving grace for us all—such a selfless act and very characteristic of my family.

School started at the end of August, and I immediately went back to work. I knew that being home alone was not something I could do. I needed to be busy. However, going back was not easy, either. My co-workers and clients mostly left me alone. No one knew what to say to me. I spent a lot of days crying at my desk, and some days I just had to leave the office.

It seemed everywhere I turned, I ran into difficulty. Once I went to the grocery store to fill my daughter's prescription, but COBRA had not yet been processed. We had been on Nick's health care coverage, and it literally ended the day he died, so I now had to pay for COBRA. The pharmacy was packed, and I was dealing with health benefits in disarray.

One of the workers knew my husband because her daughter had been his student, and she was very kind. Then one of the pharmacists who knew our story tried to console me. The kindness just made me cry so hard that I could not talk, and suddenly I felt like a crazy woman in the middle of the pharmacy bawling hysterically. It was everything I could do to get to my car and just cry alone. It took me ten minutes to calm down enough to be able to drive home. I made a quite a scene.

School Starts

As we entered fall, the support for my family continued. Sports teams had stickers with my husband's initials, groups ran the Color Run in his honor, and the food kept coming.

Brendan's football team dedicated a whole game to him, and all the kids wore orange socks and wrist bands with the number 44, the number Nick always wore playing sports. It was a beautiful and sweet gesture. It was truly amazing, and I knew he was very loved and missed by so many.

After that game, I took my daughter to a high school dance, and my son and I went home. He had a friend over, and I watched a movie alone on the couch because my family had gone to Florida. Nick's best friend called and talked about what a nice day it was.

However, I was suddenly feeling so alone in my house and just had a meltdown. I cried myself to sleep on the couch at 8 p.m. that night. All I kept thinking was that everyone else got to go home to their families, and here I sit by myself. I was angry and sad.

Grief is a terrible emotion and uncontrollable. It felt like a heavy blanket that I could not shake and, in some ways, did not want to. I was afraid that if I was not feeling pain, I would forget Nick and not love him anymore. So I wanted the pain to stay, but I also didn't.

In October, I finally sought help from a counselor who worked for a local cancer care agency. It was the best decision I made in my journey. She taught me that it was okay to have feelings of anger and everything else that I was feeling. It was a normal reaction to an abnormal and tragic event. I worked with her for 10 months and eventually stopped crying every day and being so very angry.

The winter months seemed long and dreary. I worked and took my kids where they needed to go but did not do much else. I was physically

A Kintsugi Life

exhausted from life and grief. We seemed to get a lot of snow that winter, and every time I turned around, I had to shovel my driveway. This was a reminder that Nick was no longer here, and I had to do everything. A few people who tried to console me talked about how nice it was having an "angel" watching over us.

As I was sweating and cursing, I can recall muttering more than once that I did not need an angel, I needed Nick here to help me do things, like shovel my driveway.

Looking Forward

By April of 2014, I started looking forward for the first time. It hit me that Nick would never come back, which seemed obvious, but it took me a while to come to that realization. I would always love him, but that life was gone. I needed to look forward because the past was incredibly painful. I focused on my kids and their activities and on my work. I started running a lot, probably too much, but I needed something to relieve stress.

I still could not go out socially with big groups or couples. I avoided a lot of social events and weddings. One-on-one socializing was much better for me. So, if you are reading this and I missed your wedding, party, or other event, I am sorry. Me sobbing at your wedding would not have been very pretty or joyous. I had also decided that past September that my focus needed to be on my kids and myself. I had no energy to help others at that time. It was the correct decision, even if it seemed selfish.

Signs

One of my family friends told me soon after Nick died that Nick would give me a sign that he was okay. I was tortured by the fact that he never got a chance to say goodbye and his life ended so abruptly. In hindsight, I know that was better for him. He was not ready to die and had fought so hard. Saying goodbye would have been impossible for him. I was not sure I believed there would be signs. In all my dreams about him, he looked healthy and happy.

I was always thinking—he does not know he died, and I do not want to tell him. I would wake up in a cold sweat and go through the next day like a zombie because I felt bad for him. I loved having dreams about him as they seemed so real, but it was also difficult and renewed my deep grief each time they happened.

I had no idea if I would see a sign, but on November 1, the high school where Nick taught dedicated their last home football game to him. I was running late with my kids to get to the game because a judge had scheduled a huge contentious hearing that day. It was a difficult day in court with a not-so-nice judge, but we eventually arrived at the game just a few minutes late. Nick's picture was on the jumbo screen, and they read a very nice prayer for him. Nick's brother had made orange t-shirts with Nick's initials and his favorite number, 44, that he sold at the school. I looked at the stands to a sea of orange, and it was awesome to see.

Nick had a weird fascination with the number 44. Whenever possible, it was the number he wore playing sports, and he collected bobbleheads of famous athletes who wore this number. He carved it into wood sculptures. No kidding—he loved this number, and I always thought the obsession was a bit odd, but baseball players can be superstitious.

At the end of the dedication game, his high school had won the game with a score of 44-0. It still gives me chills. His family and the principal were just in shock. I was crying so hard, I could not even speak as I left the field. But the story of 44 had just begun.

I ran a race the next summer. Bib numbers were pre-assigned and, you guessed it, mine was 44. One time I was catching a plane assigned to gate four, but an announcement told us that we were moving to gate 44. The first time Brendan's basketball team won a tournament after Nick's death, the ending score was 44.

Brendan once took a three-point shot to win a game instead of driving in for a lay-up to tie like his coach had instructed him. When I saw him after the game, his explanation was that the clock was at 4.4 seconds, and he knew he would not miss, so he took the shot. There were many times when I purchased something that my bill was exactly $44. We once bought a bottle of wine at a restaurant on my birthday and the menu said it was $48, but when the bill came, it was $44.

The number 44 comes up so much now, that I know it is Nick telling me he is okay and is watching over us. I may have doubted signs when my friend told me about them, but I certainly do not doubt it now.

Travel/Running Away

After Nick's death, I traveled as much as I possibly could. I was either coping or running away, but in the end, the reason did not matter because it was healing. I took my kids and family to a lot of fun places. We went to New York City, Nashville, Mexico, Hilton Head, Philadelphia, and anywhere else I could fit into my schedule. I would sit at work and think about where we could go next. I took all those trips that people say, "I should go do that sometime."

Well, sometime was now. My kids enjoyed being away and having fun. For a few days we could put grief on a shelf, and it was a nice release.

One-Year Anniversary

July 12 was looming, and I knew that I wanted to be out of town. My sister, my best friend, and all our kids planned a trip to Hilton Head. Two days before meeting them, my kids and I went to a PGA tournament at Greenbrier. I was blessed that one of Nick's nieces and her husband, who was a professional caddy, invited us for two days. The weather was perfect, and the resort was beautiful. It was like a dream being there and having that experience. After the Greenbrier, we met up with everyone in Hilton Head and had a relaxing week. For me, getting through the one-year anniversary was like running a marathon, and I did it. I'd dreaded that day for months. However, we celebrated Nick that week, and I had more fond memories than sad ones for the first time in a year.

My brother-in-law and I planned a memorial golf outing for Nick that August. He loved playing in outings, and I knew I needed a positive celebration for Nick's life. His funeral had seemed so sad, and to this day, I barely remember it. I wanted to do something that truly celebrated him. Almost 90 of our friends and family came to the event, and we had such a blast. It was a lot of work, but I knew Nick would appreciate it. We all needed to celebrate his wonderful life, even if it had been cut too short.

I spent several months wondering what my future would hold. The future I thought I had was completely gone. Nick and I never got the chance to celebrate our 25th wedding anniversary, and this was just unfair to us both. It is surprising how many people like to tell you how many years they have been married, and they do so proudly—as they should. But it always makes me feel like it's a contest that we lost. We were both cheated out of these special anniversaries.

I knew that, eventually, my kids would grow up and go away to college. Where would that leave me? When you lose a spouse, you do not lose just one person, you lose a lot of people in your life, and you really lose the entire life you had. That was happening to me, and I knew some of it was my fault. I was not sure I could change it, though, because I had changed. It was impossible not to. My uncertain future scared me, and I was just paralyzed by it.

The previous December, a good friend had Lasik surgery so she could see without glasses. She told me that one of the doctors who helped her was widowed, and I should meet him. Her neighbor had been friends with his late wife, and she knew his wife died young from cancer. She felt he could help me because he seemed very nice. I was not ready to meet anyone, so I told her I could not even consider this. Eight months later, my sister and my friend persuaded me to meet him. I was past the one-year mark and felt more ready to meet someone, but was not convinced entirely. Though by now, I knew I needed to think about the future and stop being so angry about the past and all I had lost.

On Saturday, August 2, 2014, Keith (the eye doctor) called me, and we met for a glass of wine that very night. I typically did not have plans as I usually declined when asked, so it worked out perfectly. I had never been on a blind date. In fact, I had not ever dated after my teenage years. I'd met Nick when I was 19 years old.

But I figured I had nothing to lose at that point. After what I had been through, how bad could a blind date possibly be? So I drove to a wine bar. It seemed surreal that I was actually doing this. I had never been to this place and was a bit nervous about finding it, which was weird since it was only 15 minutes from my house. But Nick did not drink alcohol, so hanging at a wine bar had not been part of our lifestyle.

I made it there right on time.

I walked in and saw Keith sitting at the bar. He seemed nervous, and I knew I was a little. But I had been through so much that I knew I could handle anything thrown at me. Our "glass of wine" lasted for three hours, and we shared our stories. They were eerily similar. We learned that our sons are the same exact age, born on the same day just two hours apart. His son's name is Nick, and his deceased wife's name was Tracy, my sister's name. We lived less than 15 minutes apart and knew several of the same people. I had wondered over the past few months if it would be odd to meet another person after 26 years with Nick. Well, when you meet the right person, the answer is no. It was natural and felt like it was meant to be.

I was leaving for New York and Philadelphia to visit some of Nick's family three days later, so Keith asked me if, when I got back, I wanted to have dinner. I told him that, of course, I would love to.

We talked briefly over the next couple days and set a date to meet two days after my trip. This was the first time in over a year that I was leaving town and regretting it. I wished I was home and was very excited while I was gone about coming home and having dinner with Keith. In the past year, the only time I'd felt relief from my grief was when I was not home because, at home, my grief for Nick was everywhere, and it was exhausting. I struggled with wanting to be reminded of Nick so that he was not forgotten, but it was also so painful that it was palpable.

Keith asked if he could pick me up at my house, to which I agreed. Instinctively, I knew he wanted to see my house to decide if I was normal and worth a second date. It made me laugh. We went to dinner and, just to drag out the night, had frozen yogurt after. It was the second longest dinner date of my life—we just talked for hours. When you meet someone who has been through what you have been through, the bond is instant. Truly, it was as if I had known him for years.

Dating Again

We then went on our third date, which was another long dinner and walk. For the first time in over 18 months, I started to see hope—something I was not sure I would ever feel again. I wanted hope so much, but wishing for it was scary. On that third date, Keith asked me what I was looking for. I told him I wanted the fairy tale again. I wanted to be in love and remarry someday. I was not the type to date and certainly not date around. I liked being a family, and that was my hope for the future. I was 100 percent honest and figured if that was not the answer he wanted, we were not meant to be. He liked the answers, so we continued to date.

I told both of my kids that I had been on a few dates. My 13-year-old son asked a lot of questions. If I got married, would he have to share a bedroom with Keith's son? Did I like him more than dad? Was he athletic? These things made me laugh but were his honest concerns, so I addressed each. I tried to be very open and honest with my kids so there were no surprises. My daughter took it all in stride, and her friend was more excited than Meghan was. They looked out the windows when he picked me up and remarked that they liked that he opened my car door. I never asked my kids' permission to date as I felt that was not necessary. I needed to do what was best for me and them, and I was in the best position to judge that. They were not in my shoes and were not the parent. This was my call, and I was comfortable with that.

Within a month, we were spending any free night together, which honestly was not as many as we wanted given work and our kids' crazy schedules, but we squeezed in what we could. Each date was so much fun. We went places I had never been to before, and it was an adventure. During one date, I asked if he would attend a work function with me, and his response was that anything I asked him to do, the answer would always be yes.

We decided to go to Indianapolis for a weekend in November and hit some of my favorite places in the city. It was a casual and fun weekend. It was the most time we'd spent together consecutively, and we learned that being together was easy and wonderful. My sister was convinced that Keith would propose to me, and I told her that was crazy, we had only dated for three months. He mentioned that one of his coworkers teased him about the same thing.

When we returned, I had a call in to a contractor to remodel a bathroom in my house. The bathroom was a project Nick and I had been planning before he got sick. Keith insisted that I let him do it. I was adamant that I would not have him do the work. The day after we got back, he was at my house to start demolition. He and his kids were there every night they could be to do the work. I helped where I could, but mainly made dinner and helped the kids. It was the first time that we truly felt like a family.

Keith asked me and the kids to go to Florida between Christmas and New Year's. My son had basketball tournaments that I needed to juggle, so I was on the fence. Keith was very insistent, and I was pretty convinced that he wanted to propose on the beach on New Year's Eve. I am pretty good at predicting stories, so I was just certain of this.

About 10 days after returning from Indianapolis, I met him at Mass at his parish. He asked me to come early because it was the Feast of Saint Gertrude, and he said it would be crowded. My son and I got there 15 minutes early, and Keith suggested we go into the new adoration chapel to say a prayer for Tracy and Nick. We knelt in this silent chapel for a few minutes, then he whispered that he had a question for me. He said this to me a lot, so nothing seemed out of the ordinary, and I just nodded.

Then he asked me to marry him. I was shocked and thrilled. He started hugging and kissing me, and I said I did not think we should be doing that here, much less talking! It still makes me laugh. I often wonder if the other people in the chapel knew what was going on, or were just annoyed at us breaking the rules for talking.

The rest of that day was a whirlwind. We went to his parents for brunch to tell them, and then to where my daughter was babysitting to tell her. Then to my mom's house, and my sister came over. Then we went to a friend's for a Bengals party, and many from my church had never even met Keith, and here we were, engaged! Then I went to my nephew's college basketball game and told some of Nick's family. It was a crazy fun day filled with happiness and family.

Having a Future Again

After the engagement, we had a lot to do—sell two houses, buy a house, and most importantly, bring four kids together in one household. Both of us were nervous about how the kids would react and whether they would be okay all living together. They had been through so much, and this was a monumental change in their lives. They had a lot in common, but they were also different in many ways.

Looking back, we both comment on how well it went. The kids were respectful and handled it in stride—not to say we did not have some rocky and emotional days. They all did, and so did we, but we all tried hard, and it has gone very well. Both Keith and I were very open with the kids about our feelings and acknowledged that none of this was easy. All the kids had counseling support at their schools through Fernside, and that was a tremendous help. I am very proud of all of them and grateful for their openness to the situation. I hoped that all of them loved us enough to know that we made each other happy, and they wanted that for us.

Our families were accepting of the situation, but I worried most about Nick's family and Tracy's family. In some ways, they were the most accepting of it. They truly wanted us to be happy, and although they will always be sad for the loss, they recognized our pain as well. I believe that if the situation was reversed, I would have wanted Nick to find happiness again. He was a tremendous husband, and I hope he would have shared that gift with someone else.

From the moment I met Keith, I just knew this was where I was supposed to be. When we talked that first night, his grief and pain were palpable. This makes it sound like our first date was a huge sob session, but it was positive and fun and also nice to have be able to share our journeys and pain without judgment. When we shared our grief journeys,

A Kintsugi Life

I'd really wanted to hug him tight and make his pain go away. I cannot explain how I knew down deep that he was a gift to me and our meeting was meant to be. I do not believe that life is predestined or there is a grand plan, but somehow I felt I was supposed to meet him.

Saint Pier Giorgio

During Nick's last illness, one of my friends suggested I pray to Blessed Pier Giorgio Frassati, who was on his way to becoming a saint. (He has since achieved that.) There is a nine-day novena that is prayed to Saint Pier asking for intercessions. My friend was convinced that Saint Pier would deliver a miracle to Nick and cure him.

Soon we had many people praying to Saint Pier, and I received books, prayer cards, and even CDs about Saint Pier's life. He was truly a magnificent young man who lived in Italy in the early 1900s and tragically died at age 24, but lived a life of Christ in his short years. Eerily, he resembled Nick in photographs and was known to be an athlete and very charismatic. Of course, Pier could not save Nick. I figured it was too big of a miracle to ask for.

The year after Keith and I were married, I went to a Scouting ceremony for his son, Nick, and we were in the cafeteria of the grade school that Keith and his children attended at Saint Gertrude. After the ceremony, we were at the reception, and I looked at the cafeteria walls to see about 40 pictures of Saint Pier—the same photos that I had received in books—and was speechless. Before Nick was sick, I had never heard of Blessed Pier despite being a lifelong Catholic. But here in the school that was so important to Keith, there was a wall covered with Saint Pier. It still gives me chills.

Keith kept asking me, "What is wrong with you?"

I asked, "Why do you have all these pictures of Saint Pier?"

Of course, Keith had no idea and said, "I'm not sure, who is he?"

According to a placard on the wall, Pier was a Dominican, and Saint Gertrude is a Dominican parish. When we got home, I pulled out all my books on Saint Pier and told Keith how hard I'd prayed to him. I knew that Pier could not save Nick, but I believe the miracle he did for me was to give me Keith and help me find joy, happiness, and hope again. To this day, when I need to pray for someone, I turn to Saint Pier. It is important to find peace wherever you can, and Saint Pier provides that for me.

When I first met Keith, he'd said to me multiple times that when he had finally decided he was ready to date again, the experience had not always been positive, and he'd had no idea how to go about it. He felt that God was telling him to be patient multiple times, and that was frustrating because he did not know what he was being patient for. After we met, he told me, "You were what I was waiting for, and it now all makes sense."

Grief Journey

My and Keith's relationship is different than what we each had with Nick and Tracy, as it should be. We both love deeper and appreciate each day more. Loss teaches you that. That is not to say that our love for Nick and Tracy was not deep—it was, and we both still love them and always will. But you cannot love two people in the same way. We are older now, and experiences in life have made our love richer. We are both very grateful to be where we are.

The pain of losing a spouse is not one that can really be explained or fully understood unless someone suffers it. I have taken my pain and grief journey to help others whenever I can. When I sit with friends who have lost a husband, I try to listen and be empathetic without taking over the conversation. I hope I have succeeded more than failed at this. Watching their raw pain, pain that I have had, is draining and takes me back a bit when I do it. But if I had to go through it and can help someone else because of it, I believe it would be selfish not to. I also believe that everyone's journey is unique, and there is no right or wrong way to grieve.

I wish I could say I was perfect at grief and came out as a redeemed person, but that is far from the truth. My grief and actions destroyed some friendships unwittingly. I was so angry at how unfair everything was for Nick, me, and the kids and projected that more than I should have. Some people are not forgiving and took it personally, and I cannot blame them.

I just wanted people to say, "Wow, you are right, that sucks and is unfair." But many felt I should move on and just be grateful for what I still had. They were right, but grief is not rational in many ways. In fact, it comes in waves when least expected, even years later.

Losing someone you love deeply is not something you "get over." Grief stays with you and will appear at strange times. Learning to live with grief and still be functional and happy is the goal. Some days it works, but on others you just concede and try again the next day. I have learned that giving yourself grace to have that bad day is a gift.

What I have tried very hard to do over the years is to share my experience with others going through illness or loss. I had the experience whether I liked it or not, but I learned a lot. When a friend or family member is facing a long hospital stay, I put together a very practical care package. It includes toilet paper, toothpaste, hand sanitizer, wipes, a journal, pens, lozenges, sanitizing wipes, snacks, and socks. People sometimes look at me strangely until they get to the hospital and use all of it. These were all items I took to Nick on a consistent basis during his four months' stay. I have also sat with many who suffered the loss of a husband, wife, or child. I hope that, when they look at me, they see hope that life can go forward even though it seems impossible at the moment.

In the end, my life has been put back together, but I am not the same person in many ways. I like to believe that I am a better version of myself. I am happy and living a life that I never thought was possible. Although Keith has been a catalyst for much of this, I had to do a lot of this on my own. I hope that most days, my life resembles that broken pot repaired with gold and is still beautiful, even if a bit broken, which is kintsugi, the art of taking a broken piece of pottery, repairing it with gold such that it is not the same but in some ways, more beautiful. This is a perfect analogy for my life.

I do know this: you must enjoy the journey and truly make the best of each day. You do not get them back. I wish anyone who reads this peace and healing. Remember to give grace to others. You never truly know someone else's journey.

My Eulogy for Nick

In 2013, I could not eulogize Nick and have long felt bad about that. However, I never would have gotten through one sentence at that time. He certainly deserved someone to eloquently speak about his life, but none of us could do it. His death was too tragic, and he was not ready to die. I have thought about this for many years and decided he truly deserves a eulogy, so I wanted to include it in my book.

There are so many words I could use to describe Nick, and anyone who knew him would most likely agree with me. He was such a nice person and was gentle and patient. He loved his family. He lived up to his nickname "the gentle giant" in every way possible. However, what many people do not know about Nick was that, from age 21 until his death at age 46, he suffered so many health problems. Sadly, after his first bout with cancer, he lived in constant pain. Many of you do not know this because he never told anyone.

When I asked him about this once, he said he did not want to burden others with his problems. That is such a testament to the way he lived. Despite his medical issues and pain, he lived a life of gratitude. He was happy to be alive and to have a family and a job he loved. He never complained, and he focused on the positive.

No other person has had an impact on my life like Nick. Even after his death, I tried to live up to what I felt he would want for me. I know that is for me to also live a life of gratitude. That seemed impossible in the months after he died, but I could feel him with me on the grief journey. Eventually I realized I had a lot to live for, including, most importantly, our kids. I knew I had to model behavior for them. When I realized that I needed to focus on being happy and living that life of gratitude, I met Keith. I was not looking or expecting to meet anyone at the time. It was like he was dropped out of the sky.

We both believe that Nick and Tracy did matchmaking in heaven, and we are truly a match made in heaven.

Without Nick's love for me, I would never have been able to consider loving someone again.

Nick is always with me, and I still run into his friends who tell me stories about him. Recently, one of his former co-workers made the comment that Nick loved me so much, and it felt as if Nick was there saying it himself.

I am not sure I will ever meet anyone like Nick again in my life. He was such a unique and incredible person. He was incredibly talented as an artist but was a fierce athlete who loved to win. He tried not to miss an Indiana University basketball game or Notre Dame football game, but his real passion was watching Brendan and Meghan in both sports and school plays. He also loved watching his nieces and nephews play sports. Nothing brought him more joy than a great sports contest.

For the 26 years I spent on earth with him, I am grateful for each moment we had. Here is to a life that was far too short but so well lived.

Glance of Christ

This was a speech written by our son, Brendan, and given at his senior year Kairos religious retreat.

You can tell a lot about someone just by looking at their eyes. Sometimes in class, you might make eye contact with a friend and have a conversation just by movements and looking at each other, not even using words. Almost everyone has had the experience where your teacher says you can pick a partner for an assignment and your eyes immediately meet your friend's eyes—a silent agreement that you will work together on the assignment. When you have such a close bond with someone, words aren't always needed. You know you have that when you can just sit in comfortable silence for a little bit.

I enjoy being in large groups, but I also like having conversations with people just one on one. Occasionally, I will be out with a group of people in public or anywhere, and I will meet eyes with someone and silently give a signal that I either want to go or need to talk to them. A strong relationship is needed to understand meaning just from eye contact. It shows how deep your connection runs with someone and how much you understand their personality and how much they understand yours. If you have a connection with someone like this, then that is so good. Make sure you maintain that relationship with them. As we grow older, we lose a lot of friends in our lives. Having a full connection with people is something rare, so never take it for granted. Keep those people in your life.

However, you don't always need a deep connection with someone to understand a look. You may have received a dirty look from someone. It may have been while driving, or in sports, or just anywhere. The dirty looks people give you are rude, and you should not pay attention to them.

Pay attention to the looks and eye contact you have with those people you have a deeper connection with. Those are the special looks. One of the most expressive parts of the human body is the eyes. A lot of communication can start by just eye contact.

Jesus looked into the eyes of those in His life. Some of these people may have been friends, family, or even strangers. Jesus taught all of us to love each other deeply. He looks at each and every one of us with love in His eyes. But what do you think is the response that Jesus gets when He looks at us?

Right now, you may be close with Jesus already and know him deeply, or you may be a person who wants to become deeper with Him. Someone who wanted to get closer with Jesus was the rich young man in the Gospel of Mark. The story starts with a rich young man in a crowd of people following Jesus who keeps asking Jesus how he can be certain that he will get into Heaven. Jesus tells the young man to abide by the laws and sell all his belongings to the poor. The man had been following the laws, but that was it. He did what Jesus told him to do, but he didn't really mean it. He just did it because Jesus said to, not because he wanted to. His actions showed no love behind them at all.

Jesus told us that the greatest commandment is to love one another. In any way, shape, or form, family, friends, or someone we are in a relationship with, we should love them. The rich man was unable to make the necessary sacrifices. When this rich man and Jesus locked eyes during this conversation, it was more than just the verbal conversation. Jesus asked the young man to step out of his comfort zone of being wealthy, and commit to a new life. The young man tried and abided by the laws, but it had no meaning and no love. Just going through the motions of something, but not really giving it any meaning or love, means nothing. You get it done, but it really does not affect you to the potential it could have. This is what happened to the rich young man.

Jesus also met the eyes of his close friend, Judas. Judas is one of the most misunderstood people in scripture. He was one of Jesus's chosen friends. Judas answered Jesus's call and became a follower. He was a very intelligent man and was trusted by the others in the group for finances. Judas did sin—and that was bad enough. Even worse, though, he thought that he was beyond help. He said, "I'm too bad." He had very high expectations for Jesus, and when Jesus wasn't the Messiah he expected Him to be, he rejected Jesus and His teachings. You'd imagine the eyes of Jesus and Judas meeting. Look at Jesus and how He shows us that we are never beyond the Father's love and forgiveness.

Although Judas is usually portrayed as the bad guy of the Gospel, I feel like I relate to him the most. I doubt most people I know. I don't trust myself, and I find it very hard to trust other people. I often feel that, when I do something bad or when I get hurt, nothing will make it better.

The hardest time I've been through was from fourth grade to the start of sixth grade. In fourth grade, I was in Disney World when my mom got a call that my grandpa had passed away. I was very close with him and was very surprised, as I really didn't understand death at the time. That was on a Friday night, and when I got home that Sunday, my other grandpa passed away that night. I really didn't understand how both died in such a short amount of time and was just shocked. In the springtime of fifth grade, my dad got diagnosed with leukemia. This was the second time he had cancer, the first time being before I was born. My whole life growing up, my dad was always affected by that first cancer. He had very bad Crohn's disease, blood clots in his legs, and seemed to always be at the doctors. When I heard he had cancer at the time, I thought it was normal. He was sick a lot, and this was just another thing he had. But over the next couple of months, I saw him change. It was hard seeing a person I love change so much without him being able to do anything about it.

My dad had taught at Glen Este Middle School in his early days, and during this time he was at Campbell County High School. The amount of support from everyone was crazy to me—how so many people cared about my dad. On July 12, 2013, I visited my dad at the hospital. Something had gone wrong, and he was hooked up to a big machine. My dad was a six-foot-seven, 240-pound man, nicknamed "the gentle giant." He would never hurt anybody. When I went to see him, they had him strapped on the bed so he wouldn't move. The whole day was stressful, and my mom told me to go to my basketball game because he would be okay. When I got home that night, I found out that he had passed away. My world was just flipped upside down, and I didn't know how to handle it.

My dad was at all my sporting events. He taught me how to play sports, taught me to always respect people, and—most importantly—taught me how to love. When he was gone, I gave up on everything. I thought my life was just too bad to go on. I stopped caring about school,

A Kintsugi Life

friends, and family, and I stopped caring about my faith. After all these deaths, it was hard for me to keep my faith. I just felt down all the time and like a burden to most people, and I often still feel that way.

Sometimes I really don't want to deal with any more problems in life, and just want to give up and stop caring about anything. Like Judas, I feel like I am too bad for anyone, and it is impossible to be happy after all of this. I can put a smile on my face and say I'm doing great when, really, I'm not. I'm scared of many things in life, but I am also scared of myself—scared to let myself trust people and show other people love. I want to be confident in myself and my abilities to care and love, but it gets very hard after many people you have loved seem to go away.

I realized over time that, after going through big life events like that, the road back to happiness is hard and scary. But I cannot shelter myself from everything, otherwise I will not see anything good again. I would miss out on many things. I also realized how my dad behaved. He was the nicest and most gentle person ever. He always showed people respect, no matter who they were. That long, hard battle he went through showed just how many people supported him. He was an art teacher, and he got a lot of paintings and letters from his students. After he passed, I started getting letters saying how much my dad meant to them.

My dad went through pain his whole life but was still so kind and joyful and made an impact on many people's lives. He was full of love and never let the things in life get him down. I have gone through hard times, too. I have had five surgeries in the past year. My family life has never been the same, and to this day I still struggle to be happy. Some days are harder than others, and some things in life are just very hard to get over and become normal again. I sometimes feel like I'm losing hope for something good to come along and stay in my life. I sometimes feel like my future will not be good, and I am scared.

In these times, I think of my dad. Life was hard for him, but he never stopped loving. In the time I was losing faith in God, my mom told me one of the last things he said before he died was that he still wanted me and my sister to go to Mass and never stop believing in our faith. My journey of faith has been very rocky and very challenging, but I haven't lost it. There have been many things that have happened to me that I wish had gone differently. Some things, though, like a friend or someone just leaving my life and not being close anymore, I know are okay. If someone decides to leave my life, they weren't meant to be in it in the first place. And I have faith that I will find someone that will stay.

If my dad could make eye contact with me now, he would see many emotions—some sad ones, some happy ones, and some hopeful ones. I think he would be proud of me after everything I have been through. I'm still here trying to live my life to the fullest and be happy. I hope he would be proud of me trying my best to show love to people, even if I fear getting hurt. And I hope he is proud that I still try my hardest with my faith. Occasionally I wonder what my friends see when they look at me. Do they see that I am grateful for each and every one of them, even if some days I seem like I am in a bad mood? Their eyes show me acceptance, love, and kindness. With my mom, I think when she looks at me, she cares for me, and even when I may be annoyed or upset, she is always still there, and never leaves my side. Her eyes show a glimpse of Jesus—a glimpse of eternal love.

I think about what my own gaze says. When I look in the mirror, how do I feel about myself? Do I see someone that is good, faithful, and can have an impact on people? When I look at myself, I see someone who has been through life—the happy and joyful times, and the sad times. I know God is always there for me. Even when I am alone, or even if I am happy in a big group, I know He is there watching over me. I hope when Jesus looks into my eyes, He can see I still care for Him and will not lose faith in Him, and He can see I love Him. And when I look into His eyes, I see eternal love.

Christ looks at you every day through the many people who love you. Christ may look at you today in very ordinary ways—perhaps through a silent walk, during a talk, or even during dinner. So how will you respond? Will you be like the young rich man who just goes through the motions, with no love behind it? Or like Judas and turn away, thinking you are beyond help? Maybe you can be Peter. Even though he doubted Jesus and didn't always understand, he never lost faith.

Today I believe Jesus will look into your eyes. So when He does, how will you meet the gaze? What will He say to you, and what will you respond with? You are not, and you never will be, beyond help. Jesus will always look at you with love and forgiveness, and maybe you need to open your eyes to the way He is communicating with you. I know sometimes I become blind to the love, but it is important to ask yourself

A Kintsugi Life

to try again. We will all have love—through friends, through family, and through Jesus. Keep looking for Jesus's eyes in those that surround you. And even when times are hard, know Jesus will always be there with you, and He has a plan for you. The good times will come, and those times of pain will make the good times better. Respond to Jesus's gaze, and respond with love, because He loves you.

Nick the Giraffe

By Sierra Schoening

Don't think this story is ridiculous,
When I tell you, of a giraffe named Nicholas.
You could tell he was not ordinary from the start.
Stacked up against the other giraffes he stood apart.

He started the most stout of the crew,
But then he just grew, and grew and grew.
When he finished with all the growing,
He was the giraffe worth knowing,

With a dimple in his cheek and his curly brown hair
He had a charm that was hard to compare.
His smile made the girls giggle and sigh.
Nicholas was oh, so cute, and he didn't even try.

He counted his patches, and there were forty-four
So that was his special number forever more.
He put it on his jersey, his hat, and his bat.
He loved that number, be sure of that.

He found he had many interests and talents.
Something that not everyone could balance.
He threw baseballs, footballs and basketballs.
That would be impressive, but that was not all.

Another one of his talents was art.
It was here he could express his heart.
For some, art is painting and drawing,
But for Nicholas, it was a calling.

The star of his college basketball team,
He caught the eye of pretty Kelly it seemed.
There was a romance, a wedding and such,
Nicholas' life had what seemed a perfect touch.

Then the first battle for his life was fought,
Not anything wanted or caught,
A war against cancer he finally did win,
But, boy it took a toll on him.

They dreamt of a child they may never hold,
When an angel brought a baby girl for joy untold.
Then a few years later their baby boy they did meet.
Now, truly their family was complete.

Nicholas loved sports and became a great coach.
His children and players loved him the most.
He had a special way of pushing them to excel
Even today they would be willing to tell.

His art, he went from doing to teaching.
He knew that through art you were reaching.
Reaching to understand, and to share
To touch lives and show you care.

He didn't brag about his height or looks,
Or what his sport or artistic talent took.
He saw potential in others and could bring it out
He wanted that to be his legacy, no doubt.

Illness again crossed his way,
But this time it came to stay.
His room was filled with tokens of esteem,
From his students and his teams.

He was a fighter, of that, all could see,
There were times, it seemed it could not be
That he would lose this battle,
Knowing his family's world, it would rattle.

Kelly Holden

His life touched the doctors, and nurses, and aides.
Never can we doubt the difference he made.
Even in illness his difference showed,
Through his patience and gentleness it glowed.

This may seem like a sad ending I give,
But, through this story and those he loved, he lives.
He lives on in our memories, and lessons we learned.
Gifts given from his generous heart, nothing we earned.

His greatest gift of all, was not in what he taught,
It was not in anything he sought.
Nicholas's greatest talent truly came from above.
It was simply his ability to love.

A Kintsugi Life

Two Tears

By Rachel Griffin

I had just used the restroom and was now wandering the halls of Jewish Hospital, lost and looking for the right room. Many nurses helped point me in the right direction. As I roamed the white halls, I was still grinning from the earlier car ride with my older brother and sister, Kendall and Katie. It was quiet, and I received no smiles with each room that I passed. It reeked of cleaning supplies, but the faint scent of Wendy's was pulling me into the room as I approached the door. I slipped on latex gloves and a smock. Giggling a little at how I looked, 1 walked through the door. I turned the comer until I was startled by a skinny man that looked closer to death than I had seen anyone. It was the sort of startled that forces a deep breath and a leap backward. I contained my terror, and he gave a slight smile and said, "Hey Rach." I still wonder today if he saw the fear in my eyes.

His room was covered in paintings, most of which were completed by his students. Some of his own creations were up, although he had become too weak and too aggravated with himself to paint. There were several hand-written notes stapled and stuck into boards. His room, compared to the walls in the hall, exploded with color! Orange ribbons and clouds coated every surface of his room. However, none of these things that made his room more beautiful seemed to be making him any more beautiful. I missed the way he pushed back his sweat from his forehead, using his finger and his thumb to wipe through his curly hair. He now had none. His head was not shiny like my dad's; it was dull and sad. He was the biggest, strongest man I knew. Now all I could see of him was his skeleton. The sad part is I am not even sure he looked as bad as he felt. He briefly explained to us the pain he was feeling from mouth sores. They masked the entire inside of his mouth and slid all the way down his throat. He was usually very talkative and would ask questions, but the blisters in his throat kept him from opening his mouth more often than he had to. Katie, Kendall, and I teased him about not being able to get on the bike that was placed in the front of his room. This is the type of bike one would see at a gym and think it would be the most relaxed form of exercise. It was almost comforting for us to make nm of him, and it made him feel as though he was outside those walls and in a place where we did not feel sorry for him. It was the closest thing to normalcy that I had experienced since entering his room.

We sat down to eat the Wendy's we had just bought while Uncle Nick asked Aunt Kelly to get him some apple sauce. I read the board in his room that had the rules of what he could eat. It said his food had to be bland, smooth, and cold. We could not believe that was all he could eat. As we chewed our food and chatted with Aunt Kelly, he dozed off occasionally. I watched his eyes flicker; open and closed like a butterfly's wings. It was as though he wanted to be awake but his body would not allow him. I wondered how he could be so exhausted when he had not even gotten on the bike when we teased. This disease had completely grabbed hold of my uncle, and it had him in a headlock. He could fight it all he wanted, but he was only going to lose his breath trying.

We brought him a video we had made him that had clips from all of our family members and friends telling him to get better. He was incredibly anxious to watch it. Kendall, who had made the video, told Uncle Nick we should wait for Aunt Kelly. I could see his frustration level rise as he was unable to hide his expression. He called to her, asking her to come quickly. Aunt Kelly continued to speak to nurses outside of the room. He grew enraged, crying out to her again. I had only witnessed a sweet tone of voice from Uncle Nick to Aunt Kelly. This voice was different, sort of harsh and impatient. His voice was normally so rich and warm like a big gulp of hot chocolate, but today it seemed almost whiny. We could see the annoyance on his face when he rolled his eyes and he begged to start without her. It was astonishing what four months in the hospital had done to him. It had taken its toll on a relationship I never imagined it could have.

We all viewed the video intently, tears streaming down our faces. Slide after slide, and clip after clip, I could not look at him. When it was all over we turned to Uncle Nick and he held up two fingers saying, "Two tears! I have to kick your butts twice." We laughed it off teasing him again for not having enough strength to kick our butts, hopefully mo-

A Kintsugi Life

tivating him to get better. Two tears were all he shed even after being in the hospital for several months. He only shed two tears, and not for himself, but for the people who cared for him. They were not tears of sadness, but tears of joy and thanksgiving.

As we prepared to leave, I approached him. Giving him a hug, I told him I loved him. It was not the same as all Uncle Nick hugs before. I could sense the effort, but his touch was far too gentle. It was not the lung busting hugs I used to get from him, not because he did not want it to be, but because he was not able to. As much as it hurt leaving him in the 20x20 room that he had been in for so long, it hurt just as much to stay and see him like that. I could not imagine being my Aunt Kelly, having to sit there day after day and watch him wither away. I realized that while I was home crying over homework and complaining about conditioning, he was still sitting in that room suffering. And she was still in that room, powerless, watching it all. I began to think outside myself more, and he helped me remember how blessed I really was. I learned that cancer is much more than a sickness. It changes more than just your blood cells. It changes everything, and it is much more brutal than it looks because even my big strong uncle could not beat it.

14 August 2013

COACH SCHOENING

By RILEY KINKADE

MY COACH BELIEVED IN ME WHEN I DIDN'T KNOW A THING ABOUT BASKETBALL.

MY COACH BELIEVED IN ME WHEN IT WAS TIME TO MAKE MY FIRST BASKET.

MY COACH BELIEVED IN ME TO KEEP FIGHTING FOR THAT REBOUND

MY COACH BELIEVED IN ME TO MAKE THAT 3 POINT SHOT.

MY COACH BELIEVED IN ME WHEN MY LUNG WAS NOT PERFECT.

MY COACH BELIEVED IN US AND NEVER LET US GET DOWN.

MY COACH BELIEVED IN OUR TEAM AND NEVER LET US GIVE UP

I BELIEVE EVERYTHING MY COACH TAUGHT ME.

I BELIEVE IN MY COACH.

You think you've got the best of me, think you've ha[...] me last laugh think ever[...]ing good is gone think you [...] left me broken do[...]n think [...] i'll come running back [...] you d[...] me Cause your [...]de[...] kno[...] me wrong. .....

What doe[...] kill you makes you Stronger [...] Stand a little taller d[...] me[...] i'm lonely when i'm alone what doesn[...] kill you makes a fighter footsteps even lighter.... YOU're Getting Stronger!

By Brooklyn Reese

By Lauren McQueen

A Kintsugi Life

Long Hospital Stay Checklist

- o Cough drops
- o Crosswords
- o Fun books
- o Tissues
- o Lottery scratch-offs
- o Mints
- o Notepad
- o Pen
- o Phone charger
- o Socks
- o Toilet paper
- o Toothpaste
- o Unscented lotion
- o Wet wipes

Grief Checklist

- o What makes you happy?
- o Who makes you happy?
- o Group counseling
- o Individual counseling
- o Finding a confidant
- o Engaging in activities you enjoy

ABOUT THE AUTHOR

A Cincinnati, Ohio, native, Kelly Holden earned a degree in journalism at Franklin College in Indiana and had always dreamed of publishing a novel. She had written short stories, novels, and wannabe books. But this is her first published book, which she started as a cathartic exercise to process the grief of losing her husband, Nick, to leukemia in 2013.

Since then, she has shared her journey with many and hopes this book will help others heal from tragedy and loss.

Kelly was blessed to find love again and shares her life with her husband, Keith, their four wonderful children, and a dog. She loves to travel any chance she can and spends her free time reading, attending concerts, and hosting pool parties and cookouts for friends and family.

She attended Salmon P. Chase College of Law at Northern Kentucky University and is an attorney. She proudly lives in Cincinnati, and is a fan of the Cincinnati Bengals, Cincinnati Reds, and FC Cincinnati.